Wife, Be Subject to Your Husband!
Even Though He Does Not Want You To.

by John Marshall
© 2024 John Marshall

This book or parts thereof may not be reproduced in any form, stored in a retrieval system or transmitted in any form by any means—electronic, mechanical, photocopy, recording or otherwise—without prior written permission of the publisher, except as provided by United States of America copyright law.

Unless otherwise indicated, all Scripture taken from the NEW AMERICAN STANDARD BIBLE®, Copyright © 1960, 1962, 1963, 1968, 1971, 1972, 1973, 1975, 1977, 1995, 2020 by The Lockman Foundation. Used by permission.

© 2024 by John Marshall All rights reserved

ISBN: 979-8-9877855-4-6

Printed in the United States of America

1. Eyes Right	1
2. The Great Deflection	7
3. Marriage Is a God idea	13
4. Wife, Who Controls Your Future?	21
5. God is	25
6. Elements of a Bonding Relationship	31
7. Divine Power to the Rescue	37
8. By Visual Observation, We Can Know Submissive Structure	45
9. By Verbal Ordination, We Can Know Submissive Structure	51
10. Family Submission	57
11. Why Husbands Do Not Want Their Wives to Be in Subjection to Them	65
12. Conclusion	71
13. For the Record	77

CHAPTER ONE

EYES RIGHT

EYES RIGHT

As you read this first section, you will likely ask, "What does this have to do with a book titled, "Wife be in subjection to your husband – even though he does not want you to"? But if you stay the course and assimilate the message of the whole book, I believe you will agree that this introduction is a perfect segue into the stimulating counsel of this book. As you observe the challenge within this introduction, you will notice that I am fair, balanced-minded, and not tilted to favor the husband and disfavor the wife.

Though the remainder of this book provokes the wife, this first section, Eyes Right, confronts both husband and wife.

During a military parade, soldiers march in formation. Their commanding officer expects them to keep in step with his orders and be perfectly aligned in step with each other. An officer positions himself, inspects and evaluates their marching performance. The troops have never passed this way before – by this inspector in this march. Therefore, as the troops near the location of the inspecting officer, the drill sergeant barks out the command "Eyes Right." Upon hearing this command, each soldier looks to his right and adjusts himself so that he is perfectly aligned and in step with the soldier to his right. Remember the command "Eyes Right!" It initiates the maneuver that brings about maximum marching harmony. Maximum harmony requires one to view the standard.

God requested that His people set their eyes upon His standard. *"Then Joshua got up early in the morning; and he and all the sons of Israel set out from Shittim and came to the Jordan, and they spent the night there before they crossed. Then at the end of three days the officers went through the midst of the camp; and they commanded the people, saying, "When you see the ark of the covenant of the Lord your God with the Levitical priests carrying it, then you shall set out from your place and go after it. However, there shall be a distance between you and it of about two thousand cubits by measurement. Do not come near it, so that you may know the way by which you shall go, for you have not passed this way before"* (Joshua 3:1-4). As long as they kept moving toward the standard, they did well.

God directed Moses to build an item called the Ark of the Covenant. The Ark of the Covenant was a wooden chest 45 inches long, 27 inches wide, and 27 inches high. The Ark of the Covenant was overlaid with pure gold, with a Mercy Seat – also a plate of pure gold - sitting atop it. The Ark of the Covenant contained three items, *"Now even the first covenant had regulations for divine worship and the earthly sanctuary. For a tabernacle was equipped, the outer sanctuary, in which were the lampstand, the table, and the sacred bread; this is called the Holy Place. Behind the second veil there was a tabernacle which is called the Most Holy Place, having a golden altar of incense and the ark of the covenant covered on all sides with gold, in which was <u>a golden jar holding the manna</u>, <u>Aaron's staff which budded</u>, and the <u>tablets of the covenant</u>"* (Hebrews 9:1-4).

The Ark of the Covenant reminded the Israelites of the ideas of God (Joshua 3:5-17). It was to be the one piece of furniture placed within the Most Holy Place within the Tabernacle (Exodus 25:1, 10-22). The Ark of the Covenant emphasized the person of Christ, while the Mercy Seat emphasized the purpose of Christ (Exodus 25:10-22; 36:6-9; 37:1-5; Numbers 7:8-9).

These Israelites had never journeyed across the Jordan River before. They were unfamiliar with the route to the Promised Land. Therefore, Joshua instructed the Israelites to follow the Ark of the Covenant as they crossed the Jordan River, journeying toward the Promised Land (Joshua 3:1-4).

Do you desire maximum harmony within your marriage? Then, you must keep your eyes focused on the ideas of God. Why? This is your first time being married. Even if you were married before, this is your first time being married to this person at this time under these set of circumstances. The ideas of God are of the utmost importance. Therefore, I say "Eyes Right." Adjust first to the ideas of God and then to each other.

You must remind yourselves of the laws of God. In the Ark of the Covenant, the law on the tables of stone reminded the Israelites of the laws of God (Exodus 25:10-16, 21-22; Deuteronomy 10:1-5). Husbands and wives, you must keep your eyes focused on the laws of God. He created the institution of marriage for His benefit (Ephesians 5:32-33). God designed marriage to make you holy not just to make you happy. Therefore, by design, marriage is the most delicate, durable and disturbing of all human relationships. Without divine guidance, failure falls your way.

You must remind yourselves of the provisions of God. In the Ark of the Covenant, the pot of manna reminded the Israelites of the provisions of God (Exodus 16:1-4, 31-35). Husband and wife, you must keep your eyes focused on the provisions of God, therefore, do not participate in wicked schemes to try and get "one up" on the other. As we will later discover, through the "filling of the Holy Spirit," God provides the strength and stamina to make the difficult decisions for a successful marriage.

You must remind yourselves of the chosen leaders of the wife. In the Ark of the Covenant, Aaron's rod that sprouted (budded and blossomed) reminded the Israelites of God's chosen leaders (Numbers 16:1-49, 17:1-13). Husband and wife, you must keep your eyes focused upon the head of the wife, the husband. Only now are we able to proceed to the wife.

CHAPTER TWO

THE GREAT DEFLECTION

THE GREAT DEFLECTION

What were your beliefs and feelings after reading the "Eyes Right" section? The title of this book is "Wife, be in subjection to your husband even though he does not want you to." How does reading that title affect what you believe? How did you think and feel when you read this title? Likely, your thoughts and feelings indicated that our society and even the church have wandered away from God's intended pattern and purpose for the family. And there is a need for Eyes Right. Because through society and even the church, Satan has deceived and destroyed the family. Let's begin to pay closer attention to the ideas of God.

My recent experience will indicate just how shrewd Satan has been. With a very mature, spiritual-minded, and progressively professional wife of over 25 years of an elder in the Lord's church, I engaged in a lengthy conversation about this book. She had read it thoroughly and called to give some editorial insights. Shortly after we began to talk, our conversation shifted to the poor quality of leadership that most husbands provide. We discussed the need for husbands who cast better vision and how it is almost nonexistent in most families. We discussed why men are reluctant to be visionaries and how to fix it. We talked about the generational root cause of husbands' reluctance. She recommended that I include in this book how to craft and communicate a vision to the wife. While we were talking, I decided to include that in this book. And even now, I am tempted to share that in detail, but I will not share it here. However, you may contact me through www.JohnDavisMarshall.com for detailed coaching and counsel.

What changed my mind? At 3 a.m. the next morning, as my mind replayed the previous day's conversation, I woke to a stark reality. I remembered the title of this book - **Wife be in subjection to your husband even though he does not want you to**. The title suggested that wives should do something. Why was I thinking about including what husbands should do? Therein lies the dilemma. Without realizing it, our conversation had shifted from what wives should do to what husbands were not doing and should do. Satan deflected our Eyes Right away from wives to husbands. Satan redirected even me, the author of this book, away from the trajectory of the book. Satan flipped the script. For this cause, rarely, if ever, do we fully explore the ideas of God relative to the wife's responsibilities. Please do not let your desire for solutions from the husband cloud your understanding of the responsibilities of the wife.

This deflection often leads us to conclude that we cannot expect wives to honor their subjection responsibility when their husband has shortcomings. To our detriment, this corrupt cultural perspective prevails. We buy into the myth that says the husband must be strong enough to restrain, restrict, and restore a contrary wife. In other words, husband subject your wife into obedience with niceness and niceties. There is only one thing wrong with this thinking. It is inconsistent with the ideas of God. So that you cannot truthfully say that I am partial against women, my most recent book **Husband love your wife – even though she does not want you to** scathed husbands

Corrupt culture has created and sustained the notion of a co-equal marriage between the husband and wife. By design, that can never succeed. The husband is supposed to provide guidance. You cannot guide one who is your co-equal in authority. Jesus shows us that, [5]*Have this attitude in yourselves which was also* in Christ Jesus, *⁶ who, as He already existed in the form of God, did not consider equality with God something to be grasped, ⁷ but emptied Himself by taking the form of a bond-servant and being born in the likeness of men. ⁸ And being found in appearance as a man, He humbled Himself by becoming obedient to the point of death: death on a cross. ⁹ For this reason also God highly exalted Him, and bestowed on Him the name which is above every name* (Philippians 2:5-9). Before God could guide Jesus to the cross, Jesus had to surrender His equality, saying, *"Father, if You are willing, remove this cup from Me; yet not My will, but Yours be done* (Luke 22:42). Had Jesus not surrendered His equality, He would have never gone to the cross. He honored His Father's will.

Earlier, Jesus had modeled subjection. With His parents, He was equal in worth and value but not equal in authority, *And He went down with them and came to Nazareth, and He continued to be subject to them; and His mother treasured all these things in her heart* (Luke 2:51).

What should wives learn from Jesus? Just as He gave up equality with His Father so that His Father could guide Him contrary to His preference, the wife must give up her equality so that her husband can guide her even contrary to her preference. Wives honor submission so your children can observe and experience healthy submission within the family. Wife, you are not less than your husband, but you are modeling submission for your children. Now you can understand how the husband is supposed to disciple his wife and his children. When the husband disciples his wife, he strengthens faith in the present generation, and when he disciples his children, he propels faith into the future generations. How great it is when children are born into a subjection family. Yes, Eyes Right, our parade has grown raggedy. Now let's dig deeper into this subjection responsibility and remedy this dilemma.

CHAPTER THREE

MARRIAGE IS A GOD IDEA

Marriage is a God Idea

Marriage is God's idea, so let's keep our "Eyes Right" on the guidelines He provides. First, let's establish what marriage should be from God's perspective.

Do you hear more negative or positive statements about marriage? Unfortunately, many people slander the very idea of a marriage relationship. Suspicious single folk, despondent divorced folk, and maladjusted married folk regularly ridicule the idea of a marriage relationship. God expects each believer to reinforce His ideal of marriage. Should it be that way?

God described His promises as precious, *"Through these He has granted to us His precious and magnificent promises, so that by them you may become partakers of the divine nature, having escaped the corruption that is in the world on account of lust"* (2 Peter 1:4). Using the same original word, He also described the blood of Jesus as precious, *"but with precious blood, as of a lamb unblemished and spotless, the blood of Christ"* (1 Peter 1:19). And again, using the same word that He used to describe His promises and the blood of His son, God described marriage as worthy to be honored, *"Marriage is to be held in honor among all, and the marriage bed is to be undefiled; for God will judge the sexually immoral and adulterers"* (Hebrew 13:4).

Would you speak despairingly of the promises of God? Would you speak despairingly of the blood of Jesus? Why, then, would you speak despairingly of marriage? Please reconsider and always speak honorably about marriage.

Marriage is a covenant (Malachi 2:14). A covenant is a determined and ratified agreement (Genesis 9:11-12). Because it is a determined and ratified agreement, a covenant is a binding agreement (Genesis 9:13-17).

Marriage is a bilateral covenant that obligates two people. It includes both an offer and an acceptance, which the marriage vows often express.

Observe the condensed version of the bilateral marriage covenant in Genesis 2:21-23. Now observe the expanded version of the bilateral marriage covenant in Genesis 24:1-67.

Marriage is a witnessed bilateral covenant (Malachi 2:14). Our Lord witnesses the covenant (Genesis 2:18-24). The audience witnesses it. And the state witnesses it.

Marriage is a witnessed bilateral covenant between a man and a woman (Genesis 2:19-25, Romans 1:18-32). Notice marriage as being between him/her. God affirms that fact (Genesis 2:18-25). And Jesus affirms that fact (Matthew 19:3-6).

Some have said that Jesus never taught nor said anything about homosexuality. But is that true? I beg to differ. *"When Jesus had finished these words, He departed from Galilee and came into the region of Judea beyond the Jordan; and large crowds followed Him, and He healed them there. Some Pharisees came to Jesus, testing Him and asking, "Is it lawful for a man to divorce his wife for any reason at all?" And He answered and said, "Have you not read that He who created them from the beginning made them male and female, and said, 'For this reason a man shall leave his father and mother and be joined to his wife, and the two shall become one flesh'? So they are no longer two, but one flesh. What therefore God has joined together, let no man separate."* (Matthew 19:1-6 NASB)

For human existence, family (marriage) is necessary, *"So God created man in His own image, in the image of God He created him; male and female He created them. God blessed them; and God said to them, "Be fruitful and multiply, and fill the earth, and subdue it; and rule over the fish of the sea and over the birds of the sky and over every living thing that moves on the earth"* (Genesis 1:27-28). For human behavior, marriage is normative.

Your marriage is for God's Benefit. Six times, in retrospect, God said that His creation was good (Genesis 1:4; 10; 12; 18; 21; 25; 31). But when God saw Adam's aloneness, He said that it was not good (Genesis 2:18). Whatever God says is good is good, but what God says is not good is certainly not good.

But God did not immediately provide a wife for Adam. Rather, He created the animals and paraded them in Adam's presence so that he could name them. What an intellectual giant and genius Adam must have been. The Lord put Adam to sleep, and when he awoke, he continued naming, *"Then the man said, "At last this is bone of my bones, And flesh of my flesh; She shall be called 'woman,' Because she was taken out of man"* (Genesis 3:23).

Why was Adam's aloneness not good? God instilled within Adam an inherent need for gender-complementary social companionship. Neither the animal kingdom nor the plant kingdom could satisfy Adam's aloneness.

Through the marriage relationship, God seeks to model His glory (Ephesians 5:25-32). The marriage fellowship visibly reflects God's invisible fellowship with His people. Therefore, married people should work to model God's glory appropriately.

The devil would have you believe that marriage is all about you. Therefore, when you fail to receive what you desire to receive, you abort the marriage journey. First, marriage is about God receiving what He desires from your marriage. Therefore, the married must rethink their marriage. Is your marriage more about what God gets or about what we get? Those who are seeking to become married must rethink their desired marriage. Is your desired marriage more about what God will get or about what you intend to get? In his book **Sacred Marriage**, Gary Thomas argues that God's primary intent for your marriage isn't to make you happy but to make you holy. Your relationship is more about you and God than about you and your spouse.

From the beginning, God recommended marriage, *"Then the man said, "At last this is bone of my bones, And flesh of my flesh; She shall be called 'woman,' Because she was taken out of man." For this reason a man shall leave his father and his mother, and be joined to his wife; and they shall become one flesh." (Genesis 2:23-24).* God instructed Timothy to teach the church that even widows under 60 years of age should marry, *"A widow is to be put on the list only if she is not less than <u>sixty years old</u>, having been the wife of one man, having a reputation for good works; and if she has brought up children, if she has shown hospitality to strangers, if she has washed the saints' feet, if she has assisted those in distress, and if she has devoted herself to every good work. But refuse to register younger widows, for when they feel physical desires alienating them from Christ, they want to get married, thereby incurring condemnation, because they have ignored their previous pledge. At the same time they also learn to be idle, as they go around from house to house; and not merely idle, but also they become gossips and busybodies, talking about things not proper to mention. Therefore, I want younger widows to get married, have children, manage their households, and give the enemy no opportunity for reproach"* (1 Timothy 5:9-14).

God recommended marriage for those who have a sensual appetite, "Now concerning the things about which you wrote, it is good for a man not to touch a woman. But because of sexual immoralities, each man is to have his own wife, and each woman is to have her own husband. The husband must fulfill his duty to his wife, and likewise the wife also to her husband. The wife does not have authority over her own body, but the husband does; and likewise the husband also does not have authority over his own body, but the wife does. Stop depriving one another, except by agreement for a time so that you may devote yourselves to prayer, and come together again so that Satan will not tempt you because of your lack of self-control" (1 Corinthians 7:1-5). The sensual appetite is a gift from God, *"Yet I wish that all men were even as I myself am. However, each has <u>his own gift from God</u>, one in this way, and another in that"* (1 Corinthians 7:7). Those who do not have the self-control to master their sexual sensuality should marry.

Some have attempted to squeeze marriage out of the plan arguing that scripture prohibits it. Because of *"… the present distress …"*, the apostle Paul authorized a non-normative behavior. How wise would it be to abandon the normative principle because of an abnormal situation? How much better would we be to address, seek to correct, the abnormal situation?

Within Genesis chapter one, God presented the co-dominion relationship between the male and female *"Then God said, "Let Us make man in Our image, according to Our likeness; and let them rule over the fish of the sea and over the birds of the sky and over the cattle and over all the earth, and over every creeping thing that creeps on the earth." God created man in His own image, in the image of God He created him; male and female He created them. God blessed them; and God said to them, "Be fruitful and multiply, and fill the earth, and subdue it; and rule over the fish of the sea and over the birds of the sky and over every living thing that moves on the earth"* (Genesis 1:26-28).

Within Genesis chapter two God presented the headship relationship of the male to the female *"Then the LORD God said, "It is not good for the man to be alone; I will make him a helper suitable for him." Out of the ground the LORD God formed every beast of the field and every bird of the sky, and brought them to the man to see what he would call them; and whatever the man called a living creature, that was its name. The man gave names to all the cattle, and to the birds of the sky, and to every beast of the field, but for Adam there was not found a helper suitable for him. So the LORD God caused a deep sleep to fall upon the man, and he slept; then He took one of his ribs and closed up the flesh at that place. The LORD God fashioned into a woman the rib which He had taken from the man, and brought her to the man. The man said, "This is now bone of my bones, And flesh of my flesh; She shall be called Woman, Because she was taken out of Man." For this reason a man shall leave his father and his mother, and be joined to his wife; and they shall become one flesh. And the man and his wife were both naked and were not ashamed"* (Genesis 2:18-25).

Within Genesis chapter three, God presented the curse that caused the gender combat between the male and female (Genesis 3:16). Sin corrupted the woman, taking her backstage. The adversarial relationship developed (Genesis 3:16b). This is descriptive, not prescriptive. The woman would now desire and seek to possess and control her husband. This "desire" is the same word used regarding sin's desire to possess and control Cain (Genesis 4:7). The man would rule over her. The word "rule" is the same word translated as "master" and is used to refer to Cain dominating sin (Genesis 4:7).

Neither the animal kingdom nor the plant kingdom could satisfy Adam's aloneness. God wanted Adam to have a wife. We have the exact same needs as Adam. God recommends marriage. Consider the reasons why you ought to consider marrying.

The unmarried are as significant as those who are married. The unmarried can and should significantly influence the world, even the married. The unmarried have chosen to bypass the gender-complementary social companionship allocated to marriage.

Through the marriage relationship, God seeks to manage His creation (Genesis 1:26). God deputized both males and females as custodial stewards of His creation. A husband and wife who are committed and comfortable with each other will usually rule better.

Through the marriage relationship, God seeks to multiply His heritage (Genesis 1:27-28; Psalms 127:3; 1 Timothy 5:14). A mother and father who were first husband and wife provide the best environment for nurturing and developing children. Parenting is God's first curriculum.

Through the marriage relationship, God seeks to model His glory (Ephesians 5:25-32). The marriage fellowship visibly reflects God's invisible fellowship with His people. Therefore, married people should work to model God's glory appropriately.

CHAPTER FOUR

WIFE, WHO CONTROLS YOUR FUTURE?

WIFE, WHO CONTROLS YOUR FUTURE?

Who controls your future? For anyone, who controls the wife's future? Who controls the husband's future? Who controls the children's future? Who controls the future of marriages? Who controls the future of families?

Naturally, you are apt to say God controls the future and that He controls the future of all things. At this point in the discussion, I will not disagree. However, I do have more questions. How much of your future does God control? How rigidly does God control your future? How much of the wife's future does God control? How rigidly does God control the wife's future?

Jesus believed that Satan influenced the people's beliefs: *"The sower went out to sow his seed; and as he sowed, some fell beside the road, and it was trampled underfoot, and the birds of the sky ate it up. Other seed fell on rocky soil, and when it came up, it withered away because it had no moisture. Other seed fell among the thorns; and the thorns grew up with it and choked it out. And yet other seed fell into the good soil, and grew up, and produced a crop a hundred times as much."* As He said these things, He would call out, *"The one who has ears to hear, let him hear."... And those beside the road are the ones who have heard, then the devil comes and takes away the word from their heart, so that they will not believe and be saved"* (Luke 8:5-12). Jesus referred to Satan as the ruler of this world (John 12:31, 14:30, 16:8-11). The apostle Paul called Satan the god of this world (2 Corinthians 4:1-4). Who controls your future?

You determine most of your future when you decide whom you will believe. Those who refuse to believe that Jesus is Who He says He is will die in their sin. Their future is doomed, *"Then He said again to them, "I am going away, and you will look for Me, and will die in your sin; where I am going, you cannot come." . . . Therefore, I said to you that you will die in your sins; for unless you believe that I am, you will die in your sins"* (John 8:21-24).

Adam determined his future when he decided whom he would believe. He succumbed to the enticement of Eve, his wife (Genesis 2:15-17, 3:1-6, 17-19). God banished him from the Garden of Eden forever, and he died. Also, Adam determined everyone else's future when he decided whom he would believe. Death and hardships became a reality. That death principle still operates within the universe, affecting everyone (Genesis 3:17, Romans 5:12-19, 8:22).

You determine most of your future when you decide whom you will believe. Wives determine most of their future when they decide whom they will believe. No one is hopeless. Why is this the case? Because whom you decide to believe determines whose instructions you will follow. The instructions you follow today determine the quality of life you will enjoy tomorrow.

You see this happening all the time. Parents struggle to convince their children, yet their children decide to consult with their sophomoric friends. Children determine their future when they decide to believe their friends instead of their parents. Often, they learned this from their parents. Parents determine their future when they decide to believe Satan (a lie) rather than God (the truth). Whether you believe a lie or truth significantly impacts your future (Romans 1:25). Who is the Creator? Who is the creature?

God wants you to believe Him. Believe the truth. Thus, to a great degree, you are in control of your future. Yes, wives believe it or not, to a great degree, you are in control!

CHAPTER FIVE

GOD IS!

God Is!

God is! This simple fact should settle all disputes about how, when, where, why, and how about the marriage relationship. God is; therefore, we are. We are obligated to Him. Through the wise man of old, God said, *"Remember also your Creator in the days of your youth, before the evil days come and the years approach when you will say, "I have no pleasure in them ... The conclusion, when everything has been heard, is: fear God and keep His commandments, because this applies to every person"* (Ecclesiastes 12:1, 13). And God is obligated to you. Because God is omnipotent, He has obligated Himself to you. He has obligated Himself to usher the faithful into a fruitful eternity (1 Peter 4:19, 2 Peter 3:3-13).

God is! God is simply presented to be recognized, *"In the beginning God..."* (Genesis 1:1). He makes no argument to justify His existence. He just makes His presence known.

God is! God is sovereignly powerful to be respected, "In the beginning, God created ..." (Genesis 1:1). If you disrespect Him, serious consequences will follow. He gave instructions to His creation, *"Then God said, "Let the waters below the heavens be gathered into one place, and let the dry land appear"; and it was so. ... Then God said, "Let the earth sprout vegetation, plants yielding seed, and fruit trees on the earth bearing fruit according to their kind with seed in them"; and it was so"* (Genesis 1:9-11). If you disrespect God, He will send severe consequences, *"Then the Lord God took the man and put him in the Garden of Eden to cultivate it and tend it. The Lord God commanded the man, saying, "From any tree of the garden you may freely eat; but from the tree of the knowledge of good and evil you shall not eat, for on the day that you eat from it you will certainly die"* (Genesis 2:15-17).

God is! God is surely purposeful to be reverenced, *"In the beginning God created the heavens and the earth"* (Genesis 1:1; Exodus 20:1-7, Psalms 2:11). There is a regular requirement to reverently worship Him. All possessions, positions, and praises belong to God. Therefore, to give to another what belongs to God is idolatry.

God is! God is savingly personal to be received (Acts 17:22-31). To receive Him is to follow His instructions. Wives subjecting yourselves to your husbands, even though they do not want you to, is the way to receive God and to receive good things from God.

God is! God is a Savior for His people. God saved the children of Israel (Exodus chapters 1-12), separated them (Exodus chapters 13-18), and sanctified them (Exodus chapters 19-40). The children of Israel had recently come from slavery in Egypt where they had been engulfed in gross idolatry. God separated them from the idolatry of their neighbors and sanctified them unto Himself through the Tabernacle system of worship.

Before the children of Israel came out of Egypt, worship had been centered upon and around an altar but now their worship would be centered in and around the tabernacle. God orchestrated the construction of the tabernacle (Exodus 25:8). God used two chapters to record the creation; but fifty to explain the tabernacle, its furniture, and function. He used thirteen chapters in Exodus, eighteen chapters in Leviticus, thirteen chapters in Numbers, two in Deuteronomy and four in Hebrews. Surely the tabernacle and its system of worship was and is vitally significant.

God is a Savior for His people Who makes decisions for His people. God decided that only the priests would minister service within the tabernacle and that they would come from among the descendants of Aaron, Moses's brother. God decided what they would wear when they served: Ephod (Exodus 39:2-7, Exodus 28:6-12), Breastplate (Exodus 39:8-21, Exodus 28:15-29), Robe (Exodus 39:22-26), and Outer accessories (Exodus 39:27-31, Exodus 28:39-42). Besides covering, their clothing was for glorification and beautification (Exodus 28:1-3, 28-29, 40-43). Clothing did make the man.

God decided how His majesty would be radiated. Even today, God is looking for a congregation of people who will let Him be God. For a congregation to let God be God its members must let God be God. Wives are to be an influential part of the membership of every congregation. So then, God needs wives who will let God be God. What are the criteria?

A congregation, who will let God be God, has a leader who will let God be God. A family who will let God be God, has a wife who will let God be God. For a wife to let God be God, she must willingly acknowledge God's instructions just as Moses precisely followed God instructions (Exodus 39:1, 5, 7, 21, 26, 29, 31).

Also, for a wife to let God be God she must be willing to acknowledge God's instructions that come through her husband (Ephesians 5:22-24). Just as Israel acknowledged God's instructions that came through their leader, Moses (Exodus 39:1, 5, 7, 21, 26, 29, 31, 32, 42-43).

Marriage is a God idea. It was He who brought the first woman, Eve, to the first husband, Adam. Would God make Adam a wife and provide no instructions for her? Absolutely not! In advance, God made decision for the wife.

Wives always start with divine answers rather than human questions. Take a deep breath. Don't miss the forest for the trees. Stay spiritual and continue reading. Wives, how do you feel about this so far? How enthusiastic are you about accepting God's instructions that will come to you through your husband. Or are you searching for an inadequacy within your husband that will allow you to opt out of subjection? Wives, Eyes Right!

CHAPTER SIX

THE ELEMENTS OF A BONDING RELATIONSHIP

The Elements of a Bonding Relationship

Bonding relationships become binding relationships and keep husbands and wives together for life. There exist many examples of bonding/binding relationships. The cohesive factors are the same for all. Wife, are you seeking to bond with your husband? Husband, are you seeking to bond with your wife? God provided the blueprints, *"You husbands in the same way, live with your wives in an understanding way ..."* (1 Peter 3:7).

Let's observe a bonding relationship. God brought Paul and Timothy together in ministry (Acts 16:1-3). From their first encounter, they formed a lifelong bond. Christian relationships should last. Husbands and wives' relationships should last. Each wife should seek to develop a lifelong bond of fellowship and friendship with her husband. What is the basis for this kind of relationship?

Wives build your marital relationship upon character. Character – -Character is the willingness to do right, as God defines right, regardless of the costs, because it is right to do right.

Paul and Timothy built their relationship upon character. Paul said it this way, "For I have no one else of kindred spirit who will <u>genuinely be concerned for your welfare</u>. For they all seek after their own interests, not those of Christ Jesus. But <u>you know of his proven worth</u>, that he served with me in the furtherance of the gospel like a child serving his father" (Philippians 2:20-22; Acts 16:1, 1 Corinthians 4:17).

Wives build your marital relationship upon characteristics. Characteristics – redemptive compatible qualities.

Paul and Timothy built their relationship upon characteristics. Paul said it this way, "For I have <u>no one else of kindred spirit</u> who will genuinely be concerned for your welfare. For they all seek after their own interests, not those of Christ Jesus. But you know of his proven worth, that <u>he served with me</u> in the furtherance of the gospel like a child serving his father" (Philippians 2:20-22).

Wives build your marital relationship upon chemistry. Chemistry – invisible and intangible personality connectedness.

Paul and Timothy built their relationship upon chemistry. Paul said it this way, "For I have no one else of kindred spirit who will genuinely be concerned for your welfare. For they all seek after their own interests, not those of Christ Jesus. But you know of his proven worth, that he served with me in the furtherance of the gospel <u>like a child serving his father</u>" (Philippians 2:20-22)

Wives build your relationship upon chivalry. Chivalry – courtesy, thoughtfulness, compassion.

Paul and Timothy built their relationship upon chivalry. Paul said it this way, "<u>For I have no one else</u> of kindred spirit who will genuinely be concerned for your welfare. For they all seek after their own interests, not those of Christ Jesus" (Philippians 2:20-21).

Relationships just seem to deteriorate over time. Compare your relationship now to what it was with your high-school friends. How is it different? Why?

Unfortunately, too many wives start building their relationships based on cultural conditioning rather than character conditioning from the very first date or conversation. Culture continually corrupts relationships. Character conditioning starts with character and grows through characteristics, chemistry, and chivalry. Culture reverses that order. Culture tells you to start with chivalry. Have you noticed how many females are lured into degrading relations through the chivalry of the guy? That's how drug dealers and common criminals and thugs reel unsuspecting women into a web of pain and misery. This chivalry occasionally creates some chemistry which makes women believe that they have compatible characteristics. But unfortunately, it rarely ever progresses to character.

Wives teach your daughters to view men first through the lens of their character. Evaluate him, not by how he treats her. Men will display as much chivalry as necessary to create as much chemistry as is necessary to slip your bra off and pull your panties to the side. Evaluate his character by how he treats others from whom he will never derive any benefit.

Don't give up reading. You may be asking, "How in the world can anyone do these things?" From within our humanness, we can't do them very well. However, there is divine help. Indeed, God has come to the rescue. Eyes Right!

CHAPTER SEVEN

DIVINE POWER TO THE RESCUE

Divine Power to the Rescue

The apostle Paul spoke of the potentiality of God's people. He articulated a *"can do"* statement, *"Now to Him who is able to do far more abundantly beyond all that we ask or think, according to the power that works within us"* (Ephesians 3:20). Note how that potentiality arises from the inner person.

God then moved from the potentiality of that power to the practical application of that power. He moved from a you can do to a you ought to do, *"And do not get drunk with wine, for that is dissipation, but be filled with the Spirit"* (Ephesians 5:19).

Principles from the word of God provide the best ethical and moral foundations for the family's functions. Thus, we ought to read the Bible as a "family" book before considering it as a "church" book. Apply the principles first within your family unit. Therein lie concepts borne out of divine wisdom. Therefore, from within the book of Ephesians, starting with Chapter 5 and Verse 15, we gather threads to weave the tapestry to cover the family.

Be filled with the Spirit. God exhorted the saints to be filled with the Spirit, *"And do not get drunk with wine, for that is dissipation, but be filled with the Spirit"* (Ephesians 5:18). What does it mean to be filled? What does it mean to be filled with the spirit?

The phrase "be filled" translates from the Greek verb *"plerousthe."* This original word comes in the imperative mood, meaning it is a command. For example, if a parent tells a child to "close the door," closing it is imperative; it's a command. "Be filled" (*plerousthe*) is a command that is not optional. Because it is a command, we study to understand its meaning so that we can obey it.

The phrase *"be filled"* is in the present tense. This means that it commands continuous or repeated action. An alternate translation could have been *"be constantly or continuously filled."* Did this mean that more Spirit was to be received? No. Jesus' interaction with Mary while reclining in the home of her sister, Martha, will provide insight, *"Mary then took a pound of very expensive perfume of pure nard, and anointed the feet of Jesus and wiped His feet with her hair; and the house was filled with the fragrance of the perfume"* (John 12:3). She anointed his feet, and the fragrance filled the house. One second after she opened the ointment, the odor began to fill the house. Yet, it was several minutes before the odor had fully filled the house. That did not mean that more fragrance was projected into the house but that the odor had expressed itself more completely throughout the house. After a while, the fragrance had thoroughly permeated the house. Therefore, *"be filled with the Spirit"* does not mean one receives more Spirit. But instead, it means that the Spirit expresses Himself more and more after a period.

The phrase "be filled" is in the passive voice, meaning the subject is acted upon. For example, the house did not fill itself with the fragrance; instead, the fragrance filled the house. We could say that the house allowed itself to be filled.

Therefore, the command, "be filled with the Spirit," means to continuously or repeatedly be filled with the Spirit. It does not mean to receive more Spirit but to allow the Spirit to abound, soak, and saturate your soul so that He dominates and controls. It means to experience a moment-by-moment empowering of the Spirit. This empowerment equips the saints to conquer the daily challenges of life. God informs us of that fact, *"Finally, be strong in the Lord and in the strength of His might. ... so that you will be able to stand firm against the schemes of the devil... so that you will be able to resist on the evil day, and having done everything, to stand firm. ... you will be able to extinguish all the flaming arrows of the evil one. And take the helmet of salvation and the sword of the Spirit, which is the word of God"* (Ephesians 6:10-17). The believer's strength came through what he allowed the Spirit to do.

God contrasted the results of being filled with wine with being filled with the Spirit (Ephesians 5:18). The alcohol in the wine paralyzes your "carnal center of inhibitions". You then do what you otherwise would not even think to do and do not remember doing. When you are filled with the Spirit, the Spirit paralyzes your "carnal center of inhibitions". It overpowers you with a "spiritual center of inhibitions." You then do spiritually that which you otherwise would not think to do. Neither were you able to do, *"Now to Him who is able to do far more abundantly beyond all that we ask or think, according to the power that works within us"* (Ephesians 3:20). Being filled with the Holy Spirit enables wives to live out their God orchestrated and ordered life with her husband.

Who is to be filled with the Spirit? What do those who are filled with the Spirit do? What are they to be and do after being filled? Spirit-filled people express themselves appropriately within their personal family life, the body life of the church, and within their community (civic) circles. The Holy Spirit empowers the believers to behave in the manner that is prescribed in the following verses of scripture: God addresses the believers in general and outlines their responsibilities toward one another (Ephesians 5:18-21), wives and their duties toward their husbands (Ephesians 5:22-24), husbands and their responsibilities toward their wives (Ephesians 5:25-33), children and their responsibilities toward their parents (Ephesians 6:1-3), fathers and their responsibilities toward their children (Ephesians 6:4) and servants [those who have a minority of the economic authority and social influence, being the dominated one] reciprocally toward the master [those who have majority of the economic authority and social influence, being the dominating one].

Those who are filled with the spirit begin to speak. They speak to each other, *"... speaking to one another ..."* (Ephesians 5:19). This speaking is reciprocal. But it may be simultaneous—I speak to you while you speak to me—or subsequent—I speak to you, then you speak to me, taking turns. Remember the contrast between being not being filled with wine but being filled with the Spirit. This speaking that comes from being filled with the Spirit is controlled and value-adding.

Those who are filled with the Spirit will speak in psalms. Psalms present the viewpoint of another. For example, the Psalms present the viewpoint of King David (Psalms 23; 51; 118).

Those who are filled with the Spirit will speak in hymns. Hymns tell how great someone or something is. For example, the hymn "A Wonderful Savior" tells how great someone (Jesus) is. The hymn "Nothing But the Blood" tells how great something (the blood of Jesus) is.

Those who are filled with the spirit will speak in spiritual songs, which announce the values that proceed from God's mind. For example, "A Beautiful Life" expresses the beauty of doing good deeds.

Saints of God ought to be filled with the Spirit. To be filled with the Spirit is not equivalent to *"a baptism of the Holy Spirit"*. The phrase *"the baptism of the Holy Spirit"* is nowhere found in scripture. For you are never commanded to desire or seek a baptism by the Holy Spirit. That idea is foreign to scripture. Unfortunately, many await such an experience.

Being filled with the Spirit brings about submission, *"And do not get drunk with wine, in which there is debauchery, but be filled with the Spirit, ... and subject yourselves to one another in the fear of Christ. Wives, subject yourselves to your own husbands, as to the Lord"* (Ephesians 5:18-22). God orders the wife to be in subjection to her husband. Yet, she cannot accomplish this without divine help. Therefore, the Holy Spirit provides her strength to honor the submissive structure that God has charged her to honor. To be filled with the Holy Spirit is to honor the submissive structure provided by the Holy Spirit. The Holy Spirit expresses its submissive structure through scripture. The Holy Spirit empowers wives and all believers to behave in the manner that is prescribed in the following verses of scripture. Only the Holy Spirit can enable the believer to live the God-orchestrated and ordered kingdom lifestyle. Without the Holy Spirit's empowerment none can adequately accomplish God's divine agenda. With the Holy Spirit's empowerment, all can adequately accomplish God's divine agenda.

What does submission mean by definition? The words subject, subjection, submit, and submission are all translated from the same original Greek root word "hupotasso". *Hupo* means under, and tasso means to draw up, rank, and/or arrange.

Initially, it was a military term describing a troop of soldiers who arranged themselves in formation under the guidance of their commanding officer. The fastest, most efficient way to move a formation of soldiers from one place to another is to arrange them and have them coordinate their steps according to the instructions of their commanding officer. Soldiers can literally run swiftly if everyone's steps are in sync with the direction of the officer and each other. But if they are not arranged in an orderly fashion, sore heels will result.

In a nonmilitary environment, submission describes voluntary cooperation with the guidance of another. Jesus, though superior in wisdom, continued in subjection to His parents, *"And He went down with them and came to Nazareth, and He continued to be subject to them; and His mother treasured all these things in her heart"* (Luke 2:51). What did He do? He arranged Himself in an orderly fashion under the guidance of His parents. This is a most noteworthy example of the more knowledgeable one willing to submit to the less knowledgeable one.

Submission is a God idea. God places submission everywhere. Therefore, submissive structure is a God idea. Keep your Eyes Right!

CHAPTER EIGHT

BY VISUAL OBSERVATION, WE CAN KNOW SUBMISSIVE STRUCTURE

By Visual Observation, We Can Know Submissive Structure

By visual observation, we know submission. God placed a submissive structure within the midst of His creation. By submissive structure, I mean that by created design, the animals, plants, visible materials, and invisible immaterial receive guidance from and at the expense of other animals, plants, visible materials, and invisible immaterial.

The gazelle submits to the lion to be eaten for dinner. The older, weaker lion submits to the younger lion. The younger, stronger lion, who will become the new king for the pride, destroys the posterity of the older lion and breeds for his posterity. When the gazelle is being served for dinner, the female lions and the baby lions submit to the male lion for he usually eats first.

The Bermuda grass submits and slows its growing rate in the shade of the oak tree, while the Fescue grass submits and withers to the dominance of the Bermuda grass, which chokes out the Fescue. Both grasses submit to the hunger of the gazelle, while the river's water submits to quench the gazelle's thirst.

Water submits to the heat from the sun rising as evaporation from the river to lodge in the clouds temporarily. When the cloud reaches its capacity, gravity draws the water back to the earth in the form of hail, rain, sleet, and/or snow.

All material on Earth is subject to gravity. Gravity uses its strength to hold you and me in place as we walk about on the earth.

The lights in the expanse of the heavens dominate the darkness. As God decreed, the darkness is submissive to the light, *"Then God said, "Let there be lights in the expanse of the heavens to separate the day from the night, and they shall serve as signs and for seasons, and for days and years; and they shall serve as lights in the expanse of the heavens to give light on the earth"; and it was so"* (Genesis 1:14-15). And likewise, the sun dominates the day and overwhelms the earth, *"God made the two great lights, the greater light to govern the day, and the lesser light to govern the night; He made the stars also. God placed them in the expanse of the heavens to give light on the earth, and to govern the day and the night, and to separate the light from the darkness; and God saw that it was good"* (Genesis 1:16-18).

Humans dominate the fish, the birds, the cattle, and the creeping things, *"Then God said, "Let Us make mankind in Our image, according to Our likeness; and let them rule over the fish of the sea and over the birds of the sky and over the livestock and over all the earth, and over every crawling thing that crawls on the earth." So God created man in His own image, in the image of God He created him; male and female He created them. God blessed them; and God said to them, "Be fruitful and multiply, and fill the earth, and subdue it; and rule over the fish of the sea and over the birds of the sky and over every living thing that moves on the earth"* (Genesis 1:26-28). Initially, for their food, humans exercised dominance over the plants that yielded seed while the beasts of the earth exercised dominance over every green plant for their food (Genesis 1:29-30, 9:1-5). Even a large tree exercises dominance over the grass beneath, capturing the sunlight and retarding the growth of grass beneath.

Plants reproduce after their kind. Why? Their reproduction is totally submissive to the DNA code within them, *"The earth produced vegetation, plants yielding seed according to their kind, and trees bearing fruit with seed in them, according to their kind; and God saw that it was good"* (Genesis 1:12). Their reproduction never dishonors the God orchestrated submissive structure.

Animals reproduce after their kind. Why? Their reproduction is submissive to the DNA code within them, *"And God created the great sea creatures and every living creature that moves, with which the waters swarmed, according to their kind, and every winged bird according to its kind; and God saw that it was good"* (Genesis 1:21). Why? Their reproduction (sperm and egg) is submissive to the code of their DNA. The sperm and seed never dishonor the God-orchestrated submissive structure.

CHAPTER NINE

BY VERBAL ORDINATION, WE CAN KNOW SUBMISSIVE STRUCTURE

By Verbal Ordination, We Can Know Submissive Structure

Also, submission is a human experience, for God charged the believers to obey the authority of human institutions, *"Submit yourselves for the Lord's sake to every human institution, whether to a king as the one in authority"* (1 Peter 2:13, Titus 3:1). Within its submissive structure, the government set rules and punishes those who disobey. It sets tax rates and collects them with God's approval, "Every person is to be subject to the governing authorities. For there is no authority except from God, and those which exist are established by God. *"Therefore whoever resists authority has opposed the ordinance of God; and they who have opposed will receive condemnation upon themselves. For rulers are not a cause of fear for good behavior, but for evil. Do you want to have no fear of authority? Do what is good and you will have praise from the same; for it is a servant of God to you for good. But if you do what is evil, be afraid; for it does not bear the sword for nothing; for it is a servant of God, an avenger who brings wrath on the one who practices evil. Therefore it is necessary to be in subjection, not only because of wrath, but also for the sake of conscience"* (Romans 13:1-7).

Subjection exists between the younger and the older, "You younger men, likewise, be subject to your elders; and all of you, clothe yourselves with humility toward one another, because God is opposed to the proud, but He gives grace to the humble" (1 Peter 5:5). Also submission exists among ministry servants, workers *"Now I urge you, brothers and sisters: you know the household of Stephanas, that they are the first fruits of Achaia, and that they have devoted themselves to ministry to the saints; I urge that you also be subject to such as these and to everyone who helps in the work and labors"* (1Corinthians 16:15-16).

Even more submission, *"and subject yourselves to one another in the fear of Christ"* (Ephesians 5:21). Let's explore this submission. Submission is voluntary behavior enabled by being filled with the Spirit. Submission is not about value. Submission is about order, being arranged in an orderly fashion under the guidance of another.

First, there are three contrasts. God contrasts wisdom with the absence of wisdom, *"So then, be careful how you walk, not as unwise people but as wise"* (Ephesians 5:15). He contrasts understanding the will of the Lord with not understanding the will of the Lord, "Therefore do not be foolish, but understand what the will of the Lord *is*" (Ephesians 5:17). Also He contrasts being filled with the Spirit with being drunk with wine, *"And do not get drunk with wine, [c]in which there is debauchery, but be filled with the Spirit"* (Ephesians 5:18). The Spirit impacts ignorance, intelligence, and inhibitions.

Next, there are three commands. How are they expressed? Two relate to worship, and one to the will.

Being filled with the Spirit leads one to honor the worship (Ephesians 5:18-19). The principle of worship is heaven centered ~ *"to the Lord"* (Ephesians 5:19). The purpose of worship is human-centered ~ *"to one another"* (Ephesians 5:19). Also, worship includes thankful expressions, *"always giving thanks for all things in the name of our Lord Jesus Christ to our God and Father"* (Ephesians 5:20).

Being filled with the Spirit leads one to honor the will, *"... understand what the will of the Lord is"* (Ephesians 5:17). The idea of being subject to one another is to be placed under proper authority everywhere (Ephesians 5:21, Luke 7:8).

Last, there are three contexts. The wife submits to her husband, *"Wives, subject yourselves to your own husbands, as to the Lord. "For the husband is the head of the wife, as Christ also is the head of the church, He Himself being the Savior of the body. But as the church is subject to Christ, so also the wives ought to be to their husbands in everything"* (Ephesians 5:22-24).

Children submit to parents, *"Children, obey your parents in the Lord, for this is right. Honor your father and mother (which is the first commandment with a promise), so that it may turn out well for you, and that you may live long on the earth"* (Ephesians 6:1-3).

Servants, the ones with the minority of the economic authority and social influence, i.e. the dominated ones, submit to their master, the ones with the majority of the economic authority and social influence, i.e. the dominating ones, *"Slaves, be obedient to those who are your masters according to the flesh, with fear and trembling, in the sincerity of your heart, as to Christ; not by way of eyeservice, as men-pleasers, but as slaves of Christ, doing the will of God from the heart. With good will render service, as to the Lord, and not to men, knowing that whatever good thing each one does, this he will receive back from the Lord, whether slave or free. And masters, do the same things to them, and give up threatening, knowing that both their Master and yours is in heaven, and there is no partiality with Him"* (Ephesians 6:5-9).

Some have read verse 21, *"and subject yourselves to one another in the fear of Christ"* and erroneously concluded that it was reciprocal of husbands and wives. Not so as you have seen. The submission is wife to husband, husband to Christ, children to parents, and servants to masters.

Ever since Adam rebelled in the Garden of Eden, humans have continually resisted instructions, even divinely wholesome instructions. We view instructions as nothing more than control mechanisms to which we resent with a passion. Our human depravity, inherited sin nature, which came into the world through the sin of Adam, creates an aversion to this perceived control. This control aversion runs rampant throughout the human mind. Now you understand why God required a renewing of our minds, *"But you did not learn Christ in this way, if indeed you have heard Him and have been taught in Him, just as truth is in Jesus, that, in reference to your former way of life, you are to rid yourselves of the old self, which is being corrupted in accordance with the lusts of deceit, and that you are to be renewed in the spirit of your minds, and to put on the new self, which in the likeness of God has been created in righteousness and holiness of the truth"* (Ephesians 4:20-24). Therefore, we need to be filled with the Holy Spirit.

Being filled with the Holy Spirit replaces our former carnal center of inhibitions with a new spiritual center of inhibitions that reduces our predisposition to control aversion. This explains the transformation that the apostle Paul wrote about to the Roman believers (Romans 12:1-3). This transformation is an outwardly complete and continual change in daily living. To transform is to *metamorphis* as a butterfly comes to be from the larvae and to radiate inner glory as did Jesus in His transfiguration (Matthew 17:2; 2 Corinthians 3:19). One is transformed by the renewing of the mind. By reasoning, you change your mind, which will change your behavior. As the believer undergoes alteration by the word, he also undergoes alienation from the world. Alteration by the word and alienation from the world produce a permanently beautiful believer. Only after your natural mind has been renewed can you properly assess spiritual values adequately. There is a separation of your lifestyle, a transformation of your mind, and a demonstration of God's will. Offer bodily dedication, avoid world contamination, and achieve godly transformation.

CHAPTER TEN

FAMILY SUBMISSION

Family Submission

Now to the family application. Let's examine submission in the husband-wife relationship. You should have known that, at some point, the wife's submission to her husband would sprout up. In this discussion, submission must now stand front and center and demand to be honored. Let's not fear it but rather let us believe in it. God knew that wives filled with the Spirit could better honor the divine submission responsibilities toward their husbands.

First, let's determine what submission is not. It is not a prohibitive statement to husbands. Unfortunately, this is often how the discussion proceeds. Discussions usually center on what it does not mean for the husband. I have heard it said, "It does not mean for the husband to treat his wife like a second-class citizen." While it is true that husbands should not treat their wives as second-class citizens, the principle of this passage does not legislate a prohibition for the husband.

It is not a solicitive statement to husbands. God was not trying to get husbands to engage in a particular behavior when He ordained submission for the wife.

It is not even a statement to husbands. They do not need to know that this statement is in scripture. It is not even directed to husbands.

God addressed this command to wives. It is an initiative statement to wives. It sought to initiate the wives into doing something. This verse confronted the wives' initiative, not the husbands' prohibitive. Always remember that and rise to correct the misdirection miscued by this passage. It's not about your husband's actions or inactions, his abilities or inabilities; this passage is to wives; it's about you. God is speaking to you, so are you submissive enough to listen to Him? When you are respectfully submissive, you are honoring your husband and upholding God's word and His blueprint for the family.

We can better prepare to honor this submission by again looking at how God orchestrated a submissive structure within the design fabric of the universe. He created lights. Those lights separated day from night and hoisted themselves for signs, seasons, days, and years, *"Then God said, "Let there be lights in the expanse of the heavens to separate the day from the night, and they shall serve as signs and for seasons, and for days and years; and they shall serve as lights in the expanse of the heavens to give light on the earth"; and it was so. God made the two great lights, the greater light to govern the day, and the lesser light to govern the night; He made the stars also"* (Genesis 1:14-16). God positioned two great lights with divine calibrated precision: the sun and the moon. Of the two, the sun distinguished itself as the great light and governed the night. At the same time, the moon submitted itself as the lesser light and governed the night. In addition, He systematically aligned the stars (Genesis 1:16).

Many years after the creation, Jacob, the grandson of our father of faith, Abraham, perceived this relationship between the sun, moon, and stars to indicate God's submissive structure. Jacob's son, Joseph, the dreamer boy, dreamed that the sun, moon, and stars bowed down to him. Jacob interpreted the son's dream to signify him as the father, the moon to signify Rachel, the mother, and the stars to signify his other eleven sons, *"Then Joseph had a dream, and when he told it to his brothers, they hated him even more. He said to them, "Please listen to this dream which I have had; for behold, we were binding sheaves in the field, and behold, my sheaf stood up and also remained standing; and behold, your sheaves gathered around and bowed down to my sheaf." Then his brothers said to him, "Are you actually going to reign over us? Or are you really going to rule over us?" So they hated him even more for his dreams and for his words. Then he had yet another dream, and informed his brothers of it, and said, "Behold, I have had yet another dream; and behold, the sun and the moon, and eleven stars were bowing down to me." He also told it to his father as well as to his brothers; and his father rebuked him and said to him, "What is this dream that you have had? Am I and your mother and your brothers actually going to come to bow down to the ground before you"* (Genesis 37:5-11)? Right from the start, God orchestrated and illustrated a submissive structure within the social order of the universe. Literally speaking, the moon submitted itself to the sun, and the stars also submitted themselves to the sun. Figuratively speaking, the sun represented the husband (father), while the moon represented the wife (mother), and the stars represented the children.

Submission is not a preferred human dynamic. Submitting does not come automatically. It only comes intentionally with disciplined practice. We need divine help. Therefore, God provided the Spirit to enable us to honor the assignment.

Let's examine this husband-wife submission dynamic. Let's apply the concepts learned earlier to the marital relationship.

How are we best to understand and honor God's submissive structure? We are better able to honor submissive structure when we are filled with the Holy Spirit of God (Ephesians 5:19). After admonishing the believers to be filled with the spirit, God charged spirit-filled wives to subject themselves to their own husbands. Spirit-filled wives can and will respect their husbands (Ephesians 5:33). Wives demonstrate their respect by submitting themselves (arranging themselves in an orderly fashion) to their own husbands (Ephesians 5:22). Thus, submitting is simply arranging oneself in an orderly fashion under the guiding influence of her husband.

Wives submit to their husbands because Jesus is Lord (Ephesians 5:21-24). But, you say, "I just cannot submit." When you are filled with the Holy Spirit, you will be able to submit because it is no longer "you/I" but rather "He who dwells" (Galatians 2:20) inside of you who always does God's will.

You and I have heard people say that respect must be earned. We have likely heard some say that the right to subjection must be earned. Unfortunately, when we drill deeper into the equation, we will likely find that a wife who prefers not to submit will excuse herself by saying, my husband isn't worthy or has not earned that right. Submit not because the husband has earned respect but because you are crucified with Jesus and surrendered to His Lordship. God cleaned that up so we will not fall into this secular trap. He admonished wives to submit to their husbands even while their husbands were nonbelievers, *"In the same way, you wives, be subject to your own husbands so that even if any of them are disobedient to the word, they may be won over without a word by the behavior of their wives as they observe your pure and respectful behavior"* (1 Peter 3:1-2). Do you believe that a husband, while being disobedient to God's very word, has earned the right of submission? Absolutely not! Submit because it is the will of God.

Submitting is a heart decision to agree with God. Wives submit themselves. Husbands do not submit their wives. Submitting is an internal decision on the part of the wife. It is not an external demand by the husband. Even when a husband is less than ideal, submit. Jesus is your example. Though Jesus suffered at the hands of those who wrongfully judged him, he never sinned. He kept entrusting himself to the One who would righteously judge him (1 Peter 2:22-23). His example provided a pattern of peace for wives (1 Peter 2:21-3:1). For Wives, your marital relationship should be progressively peaceful when you follow God's directives. Peace is the absence of distress that is caused by sin. Where will His directives lead? They will lead away from distress.

Consider your conduct (behavior) (1 Peter 3:1-2). No. Not the *"I will if and when he does"* kind of verbal combat. Be in submission even to a non-believing husband who has not been persuaded by the verbal declaration of truth. Your submissive behavior may prove to be your most powerful form of persuasion.

Consider your cosmetics, *"Your adornment must not be merely the external— braiding the hair, wearing gold jewelry, or putting on apparel; but it should be the hidden person of the heart, with the imperishable quality of a gentle and quiet spirit, which is precious in the sight of God"* (1 Peter 3:3-4). The word adornment comes from the Greek word *kosmos* from which we get our English word cosmetics. Kosmos refers to the harmoniously arranged universe with its planetary bodies (sun, moon, stars). Thus, your cosmetics seek to be a harmonious makeup arrangement (lipstick, eye shadow, etc.) upon the body. Scripture does not prohibit cosmetics but places the point of main emphasis on internal beauty more than on external beauty (John 6:27).

Contrast your efforts for internal beauty with your efforts for external beauty. In our *shop-till-you-drop* culture, when so many are in ready, set, charge mode, it becomes easy to emphasize externals and downplay internals. Don't think for a minute that God opposes beauty. For when He created the universe, He created trees for eye appeal, *"Out of the ground the Lord God caused every tree to grow that is pleasing to the sight and good for food; the tree of life was also in the midst of the garden, and the tree of the knowledge of good and evil"* (Genesis 2:9). Externals should be in the background while internals should be in the foreground.

God wants you to evaluate yourself. Wives submit to their husbands because God placed husbands as heads (Ephesians 5:22-24). Submitting to him as the guiding influence lends itself to efficient and effective function within the family.

Holy Spirit-filled wives will learn how to honor God's submissive structure within the family (Ephesians 5:19-24). What is this submission stuff all about?

What **does** submission mean for the wife? It defines a wife who exhibits and models cooperation for her children. She teaches her children to respect their father and position the family for its most significant progress. Submission is modeled by respecting the husband's guiding influence and trusting his God-given wisdom as a leader. Therein, the wife voluntarily cooperates with the guiding influence of her husband just as Jesus did with His parents (Luke 2:51). Just as Jesus might have been more knowledgeable than His parents, there are times when the wife is more knowledgeable than her husband, but submission requires voluntary cooperation independent of who's more knowledgeable. Yes, the more knowledgeable might need to be willing to submit to the less knowledgeable. It is a great teaching moment for children.

CHAPTER ELEVEN

WHY HUSBANDS DO NOT WANT THEIR WIVES TO BE IN SUBJECTION TO THEM

Why husbands do not want their wives to be in subjection to them

Why do so many husbands not want their wives to be in subjection? For the wife to be in subjection, the husband must provide a crucial guiding influence. Yes, he must lead and guide, understanding his significant role in the family's spiritual journey.

Many husbands are unmotivated. It is so easy just to let the wife do it. Men cop out by thinking and saying, "My wife is so much better at this than I am." This is not the way God intended it to be. They do not want to be responsible for crafting a vision for the family. They would instead share an opinion or support the guidance provided by their wives. How unfortunate. This is not the way God designed it.

Many husbands are uneducated, and they are often uneducated to lead. This does not mean that they are not academic. It just means they have not learned the ways of family guidance.

He does not know that he is to lead. His father is absent from his life, and no one has ever taught him that he is to guide his wife and family. When he first hears this, it seems so mysteriously foreign that he does not believe it is true. Once he is convinced that he should lead, he does not know how. Ignorance paralyzes his guidance.

Before the husband can adequately guide, he must have decided who or what guides him. Hopefully, his God-given wisdom guides.

Many husbands are afraid to provide guidance. They are afraid of failure. They are afraid that their wives will rebel. When the wife rebels and refuses to allow her husband to guide her, she not only bruises his masculine ego but also significantly undermines his subsequent authority, making him feel powerless. He loses all authority. Therefore, wives convince your husbands that you will never rebel, unless he is attempting to guide you contrary to a clear principle of scripture (Acts 5:29).

Husbands who are trying to walk with God are more fearful than husbands who are not. They know and have likely experienced that to get their way, wives will withhold sex. This is extremely painful for the Christian husband, for he has no other sex option but to wait till his wife decides to return to being a nurturing, intimate wife. The non-Christian man has options: he "beats" his wife into subjection, or he relies on his attractive coworker to graciously gratify his social and biological needs.

Too many husbands do not want to be held accountable for deciding and designing their leadership roles; thus, they do not want their wives to be subjected to them. When wives submit, husbands must lead.

A word to the wives. You can never improve your relationship by withholding sexual gratification from your husband. You may occasionally win the battle but you will always lose the war. Do not buy the myth that a woman cannot give of herself until after she has experienced personal fulfillment being made to feel special. Prostitutes prove that to be a false claim.

Where did we get off track? We got off track in the first grade. The little boys said to the girl, Are you going to give me some. The girl grows up believing that when she engages in sexual intercourse she is doing the boy a favor by giving him something. No one ever challenges that thinking. Now as a wife she continues to believe that. So she thinks she must have a reason to give him some. If there is no reason, she feels justified in withholding. This notion is supported by a conversation in one of my counseling sessions. The wife declared that she thought that sex was a reward for her husband. When he did not fulfill her expectations, he failed to receive a reward. As an example, she stated that if he was supposed to pick up bread on the way home from work and he forgot, she was justified in depriving him of sexual pleasures that night. I had to inform this woman that she was guilty of infidelity, *The husband must fulfill his duty to his wife, and likewise also the wife to her husband. The wife does not have authority over her own body, but the husband does; and likewise also the husband does not have authority over his own body, but the wife does. Stop depriving one another, except by agreement for a time, so that you may devote yourselves to prayer, and come together again so that Satan will not tempt you because of your lack of self-control* (1 Corinthians 7:3-5). Wives when you deprive your husbands, you set them up for moral failure. You cannot set your husband up for failure and remain guiltless. Wives decree now that you will never deprive your husband of sexual gratification and that you will never go to bed angry (Ephesians 4:26-27).

CHAPTER TWELVE

CONCLUSION

Conclusion

<u>Before Getting Married</u>
Before getting married, read my book, "A Queen in Search of a King – go ahead and ask Him for a date."

Start now preparing yourself to select a husband who will listen to God. This kind of man will guide you and the family far better than one who does not listen to God. But you ask, where are the men with God-given wisdom? Let me suggest how to identify. Make a list of your core values ~ the fundamental beliefs that guide your beliefs and behavior toward right and wrong.

Start reading and meditating upon the Proverbs, Solomon's wisdom Literature. Study one chapter per month. Write a specific note about the verses that you do understand. Do not fret over the verses that you do not understand. For the time being, skip over the portions of the verses that you just cannot comprehend. Eventually through participation and meditation, you will grow to understand, "Consider what I say, for the Lord will give you understanding in everything" (2 Timothy 2:7).

Whenever you meet a man seek to find out what his core values are. If your values are compatible share with him your values. If your values are incompatible there is not likely any need for further dating consideration. However, you may offer a better set of values for consideration. If he rejects, there is no need for further dating consideration. If he accepts, share your values. There may be the possibility of a spiritual connection. Once the values are out in the open, entice him to read and meditate upon the Proverbs with you. If he refuses, then there is no need for further dating consideration.

You say that will run men away. That is exactly what you want to do. Remember you are sifting, not sorting. Therefore, you want to run all men away except the one who is for you.

After Getting Married
After getting married read my books, "A Queen in Search of a King – go ahead and ask Him for a date," "The Power of the Tongue - what you say is what you get," and "Good and Angry – personal guide to anger management."

For some, subjection seems like the wife is to blindly follow a sightless husband. But absolutely not; to the contrary. Wives, share your emotional, intellectual and spiritual perspectives. Then expect your husband to guide. Therefore, you should want to know:

Does my husband listen to God?
How well does he listen to God?

What are the indicators that he listens to God?
Does he listen till he hears from God?
Does he listen intending to obey God?

Wives must cooperate with healthy attitudes and actions, though they may and often should ask, "Where are you guiding me?" What is our destination? How will the journey be? The wife does not become guilty of insubordination by asking where she's being led. You can, and you must ask.

Submission is voluntary. Submission is not about value. Submission is about order – arranged in an orderly fashion under the guiding influence of another.

Observations

1- If you are subject to government and employer [who thinks nothing of you], why are you so aggravated at being subject to your husband [who thinks the world of you]? With a smile you will introduce your ruthless supervisor as your boss and frown at the very thought of being in subjection to your own husband. Why?

2-To the extent that the idea of submission aggravates you, it is to that extent that your sin nature overrules your spiritual nature (Romans 8:8). You are yet afflicted by the Edenic curse (Genesis 3:16). The curse is real, and it really afflicts you.

3-The solution is not to eliminate, abdicate, or usurp the God-preferred submissive structure but to arrest your sin nature. Allow the Holy Spirit of God to subdue your sin nature. The death of Jesus removes us from this and all curses of sin. Apply His blood and enjoy His freedom.

4-Subjection is the most efficient and effective structure.

Challenge

God wants you to voluntarily place yourself in an orderly fashion under the guiding influence of your husband. List three (3) ways in which you express your submission for your husband. Many husbands do not want their wives to be submissive.

God intended for each wife to submit herself to her own husband (Ephesians 5:22). Holy Spirit filled wives will submit themselves to their own husbands (Ephesians 5:19-24). What is this submission stuff all about? Answers to questions: Wife submit to your husband.

What if my husband misses my preference? For example, what if he wants to go on vacation in New York during the winter, but I want to go to Florida, where it is warm? Pray, give him your husband all of your preference information, and allow him to guide you. Trust God to change his mind or go on vacation believing that God has a purpose for you in New York during the winter. Who knows how many wonderful experiences your family has missed because you were outside the will of God?

What if my husband does not do what I believe is in my best interest? Does God always do what you believe is in your best interest? Delay selfishness and trust your husband as you trust God (Colossians 3:19). Model trust and submission for your children. Who will they learn these traits from? Wives refuse to submit to their husbands at home and go to a job and do everything their supervisor asks.

How can that be better for us? We have never functioned like that. We do everything 50/50. You may have a career, children, and contentment in the home. However, God may have wanted you and your children to do great things, but your husband never saw the vision, or you failed to cooperate with the vision; thus, you led mediocre lives. Only eternity can tell how much was missed because of violation.

Observation
Men need to know that their wisdom is wanted, welcomed and believed to be worthwhile for the wife. Why would you bring a husband into your relationship if you do not believe that God has given him wisdom? Why would you bring a husband into your relationship if you do not believe that God has given him wisdom for you? Why would you not want and welcome as worthwhile the God-given wisdom of the husband you have married?

Do not wish to circumvent his wisdom. Do not seek to circumvent his wisdom. Trust the God-given wisdom that your husband has received.

Men wish women knew how to develop the capacity to appreciate their sanctification and glorification above all else. Therefore, women stop dismissing men and blaming them for your inappropriate behavior. Stop saying that when men do what they are supposed to do, women will do what they are supposed to do. When did God condition one person's correct behavior contingent upon another person's correct behavior (1 Peter 3:1-2)? Never!

Stop looking for perfection while you classify the man's wisdom as inadequate. When we do not wish to accept the authority principle, we work to invalidate the authority person. People work overtime to invalidate God as the Creator so that they do not have to accept Him as the Administrator.

Too many husbands do not want to be held accountable for deciding and designing their leadership roles; thus, they do not really want their wives to be subjected to them. When wives submit, husbands must lead.

Eyes Right before the marriage begins! Eyes Right all along the journey until death or the rapture.

CHAPTER THIRTEEN

FOR THE RECORD

FOR THE RECORD

BECOME SAVED – The Basis of Salvation
The first mention of blood was Abel's (Genesis 4:10). The last mention of blood was Jesus' (Revelation 19:13). In between times, God sprinkled blood around, about, and all upon His people (Exodus 24:6-8, 29:15-21).

Scripture reveals that the blood of Christ cleanses us from the guilt of sin as we are born into the family of God (1 Peter 1:17-19; Revelation 1:4-6). Grace made the cleansing power of the blood available, but faith activates it (Exodus 12-14; 1 Corinthians 10:1-4).

Scripture reveals that the blood of Christ cleanses us from the guilt of sin after we are born into the family of God (1 John 1:5-2:1; Ephesians 1:3-8). Forgiveness is durative even for those who are not living a perfectly sinless life.

God wants you to think thoroughly about the blood of Jesus. Never ask, "Can God forgive the sinner?" On the basis of the blood of Jesus, God can forgive sinners. Never ask, "Will God forgive the saint?" On the basis of the blood of Jesus, God will forgive saints. God wants you to celebrate the power of the blood (Exodus 12:13, 1 Corinthians 10:1-4; John 19:34). God is a bloody God. The bible is a bloody book. Believers, God's people, are a bloody people.

Moses negotiated with Pharaoh for the release of the Israelites from captivity. Only after the Passover, the tenth plague, did Pharaoh release the Israelites. But, as they traveled toward the Promised Land, Pharaoh changed his mind and pursued after them.

With his army, Pharaoh sandwiched the Israelites against the Red Sea (Exodus 14:5-9). God provided salvation (Exodus 14:13-14). Salvation was a military term describing an escape from a position of danger to a position of safety.

Salvation is a deliverance from an old relationship. In their old relationship, they served Pharaoh (Exodus 1:8-14; 5:1-14). In our old relationship, we served sin (John 8:34, Romans 6:16-17). Actively, we do that which the Lord does not authorize (1 John 3:4). Passively, we refuse to do that which the Lord does authorize (James 4:17; Luke 12:47-48).

Salvation is a deliverance from an old relationship to a new relationship. In their new relationship, they served Moses. In our new relationship, we serve righteousness (Romans 6:16-18). Actively, we do that which the Lord authorizes. Passively, we refuse to do that which the Lord does not authorize.
Of the several types of salvation the Bible speaks of, the relationships delivered from and to may differ; however, the principle of the process of the deliverance remains the same. Salvation takes place according to an authorized process.

> A) For their salvation from Pharaoh:
>   1) The Lord, who provided salvation, responded.
>   2) The Lord's spokesperson, who informed them of the salvation, responded.
>   3) The endangered people, who needed to receive the salvation, responded.

God provided this salvation for them and Paul called it a baptism (1 Corinthians 10:1-2). This process was: (a) necessary, (b) different, (c) humanly illogical, but (d) successful.
  B) For our salvation from sin:
   1) The Lord, who provides salvation, has responded. He sent Jesus as your sin substitute.
   2) The Lord's spokesperson, informs you of salvation.
   3) The endangered people, you, who need to receive this salvation, need to respond.

Salvation from sin is a deliverance from an old relationship to a new relationship by way of an authorized process. This process was: (a) necessary, (b) different, (c) humanly illogical, but (d) successful. Salvation is not a biological, economical, or racial issue, but a scriptural issue (2 Timothy 3:15).

The blood was shed (Exodus 12:1-28). Yet, Israel had not been freed from their slavery to Egypt. Why? There was something they needed to do. They had to go through the waters of baptism (Exodus 14:21-25, 1 Corinthians 10:1-2).

The blood of Jesus has been made available. Unfortunately, all are not saved. Why? Reconciliation was accomplished at the cross but is appropriated at conversion (baptism). Those who are unsaved have not come to enjoy the appropriation of the blood of Jesus. For example: The college student's school loan for the year is accomplished when the university approves it, but the loan is appropriated at the beginning of each semester when the student registers. Your earnings are accomplished each hour, but appropriated when you receive the paycheck.

Many are unsaved because they have no faith response to the resurrection of Jesus. Salvation is accomplished for them, but not yet appropriated to them. Salvation will be appropriated to them when they engage in the behavior (baptism) that leads to salvation.

First Implementation of God's Plan of Salvation (Acts 2)
The law of "first mention" may be said to be the principle that requires

you to go to that portion of the Scripture where a doctrine is mentioned for the first time and to study the first occurrence of the same in order to get the fundamental inherent meaning of that doctrine. When you thus see the first appearance, which is usually in the simplest form, you can then examine the doctrine in other portions of the Word that were given later. You shall see that the fundamental concept in the first occurrence remains dominant as a rule and directs (interprets) all later additions to that doctrine.

HEAR THE GOSPEL - In order for you to be saved, you must hear the gospel. The gospel is the good news of the availability of the salvation that has been provided for by the grace of God and the sacrificial blood of Jesus. The death, burial, and the resurrection of Jesus are the certified facts of the gospel (1 Corinthians 15:1-4). Hearing the gospel is one of the certified obedience requirements of the gospel.

Acts 2:1-4: The apostles preached a Holy Spirit-directed sermon. This was the first sermon preached to unsaved people after the resurrection of Jesus. Therefore, we can apply the "law of first mention".

Acts 2:6-8: In their own (native) language, the people heard the Holy Spirit-directed sermon.

Acts 2:29-33: The people heard the certified facts (death, burial, resurrection) of the gospel of Jesus Christ.

Acts 2:36-37: Hearing the fact of the resurrection of Jesus, the Man they had crucified, pierced their heart. Yes, this sermon irritated their conscience.

BELIEVE THE GOSPEL - In order for you to be saved, you must believe the gospel. To believe the gospel is to intellectually and emotionally embrace the facts of the death, burial, and resurrection of Jesus.

Acts 2:12-16: Though they understood verbally what was said, at first some did not know the meaning of the message experience. Therefore, they asked, "…What does this mean?" Some of the people suggested that the apostles were experiencing drunkenness. Therefore, they said, "…They are full of sweet wine."

Acts 2:22-24: Though they did not initially know the meaning of this message, when they were reminded of the ministry of Jesus, they could not help but believe their knowledge of what God had done through Jesus.

Acts 2:32-33: God had raised Jesus from the dead and exalted Him. Again,
they were reminded of what they had already observed "...we are all witnesses. ... this which you both see and hear."

Acts 2:37: Because they believed that God had raised up to life the very Man they had put down to death, the preached word pierced their heart, and irritated their conscience.

Acts 2:41: Because they had come to believe that Jesus was the Son of God, they received the word.

REPENT OF SIN - In order for you to be saved, you must repent. Repentance is your change of heart that takes place in your mind (Matthew 21:28-32). In repentance, you change your allegiance (Acts 17:30, 26:19-20). Repentance is a resetting of your allegiance. It is a resetting of your allegiance from your selfish self to the Savior.

Acts 2:38: The Holy Spirit led the apostle Peter to command the people to repent of having opposed God, "Peter said to them, repent..."

Acts 2:41-42: Earlier, they rejected the word and crucified Jesus. But now, they are receiving the word and embracing Jesus as the Son of God. This change of heart indicates their repentance.

CONFESS THAT JESUS IS THE SON OF GOD - In order for you to be saved, you must confess. What does it mean to confess? Confess is translated from a compound word (homlogeo) that means to speak the same. Therefore, to confess is to admit (John 1:20, 12:42). To confess is to acknowledge (Romans 10:9, 14:10-12, Hebrews 13:15). Confess means that you agree at heart and speak the same thing as another (1 John 1:10).

Acts 2:37: God said that Jesus is His Son (Matthew 3:16-17). Therefore, the people must admit that Jesus was the Son of God. By asking, "what shall we do", they admitted that they had come to believe the gospel that had been preached. Yes, they agreed with and acknowledged the truth of the fact that Jesus was the Son of God.

BECOME BAPTIZED – In order for you to be saved, you must be baptized. Baptism is your faith response of being buried in water in response to the fact that Jesus Christ is the Son of God (Acts 8:12; 37-39; 1 Peter 3:21). Baptism is mentioned some 92 times in the New Testament. Interestingly, Jesus began His earthly ministry being baptized of John in the Jordan River (Matthew 3:13-17) and concluded His ministry by commanding His apostles to baptize those who would become His disciples (Matthew 28:19-20). **Obviously, baptism is essential.**

Acts 2:38: The Holy Spirit led the apostle Peter to command them to *"... be baptized in the name of Jesus Christ for the forgiveness of our sins..."* The purpose for which they were to become baptized harmonized with the earlier statement of Jesus (Mark 16:16). This was the first time the apostles had ever taught about baptism. This was the first time the apostles had ever told a person to become baptized. Though Jesus had taught the relationship between baptism and salvation, this was the first time the apostles had ever taught the inherent relationship between baptism and salvation. The "law of first mention" must be considered in this instance.

Acts 2:40-42: Obviously, those in the audience believed that there existed an inherent relationship between baptism and salvation, for 3,000 people who received His word were baptized that same day.

BECOME SAVED – The Relationship Between Baptism and Salvation

Read: Mark 16:16
Where did Jesus place baptism; before salvation or after salvation?

Why is there so much confusion on the subject of baptism? An intellectual "exegesis" [reading out of] of scripture rather than an emotional "eisegesis" [reading into] of scripture peels away most of the layers of confusion. Let's proceed.

The Holy Spirit could not come until after Jesus had risen from the dead and ascended to heaven (John 16:7). Some 40 days after Jesus had risen from the dead, the Holy Spirit was yet to come (Acts 1:1-8). The Holy Spirit came on the day of Pentecost (Acts 2:1-4).

The Holy Spirit revealed the message of truth to those who wrote scripture (Ephesians 3:1-5, 2 Peter 1:21). The apostle Peter spoke the words of Acts 2:38 before Matthew, Mark, Luke, and John wrote the words contained in their Gospels. Being from regions beyond Jerusalem, most of those who heard the words of Acts 2:38 had not heard Jesus speak (Acts 2:9-11). Even those who had heard Jesus speak had failed to understand His message; therefore, they crucified Him (John 20:30, Acts 3:29).

Historically, the Jews had offered sacrifices with an understanding that they would invoke the forgiveness (appeasement) of God. Even on Pentecost, they believed that they needed to respond in order to receive forgiveness of God. Therefore, they asked, "What shall we do" (Acts 2:37).

Peter had just preached a persuasive sermon designed to convince the audience that Jesus was the Christ and Lord (Acts 2:36). Obviously, some who heard, also believed, for their hearts were pricked (Acts 2:37). Hearts are never pricked until belief comes. In addition to believing, they asked what to do. In other words, they were now asking, "After believing what (else) shall we do? If they had been forgiven [saved] just by believing, then Peter should have told them so. Otherwise, he accommodated their false belief about doing something, in addition to believing in order to be saved.

In the past, they had killed and offered an animal in their effort to receive forgiveness of sins. Peter informed them that no longer would they have to kill a lamb. The Lamb (Jesus) had already been slain. They must now repent and be baptized to embrace the death of Jesus.
Only after Jesus had been raised from the dead did He teach of the cause and effect relationship of baptism with salvation.

But what about Romans 10:9-10? Let's set the stage.

1. Those to whom the apostle Paul addressed this letter were called and had become saints (see Romans 1:6-7).

2. They had died to sin (see Romans 6:2).

3. They had been baptized into Christ and His death (see Romans 6:3).

4. They had been raised from the dead to walk in the newness of life (see Romans 6:4).

5. They had become united with Jesus (see Romans 6:5).

6. Their old self had been crucified with Christ (see Romans 6:6).

7. They had obeyed from the heart the doctrinal teachings (see Romans 6:17).

8. They had been freed from sin (see Romans 6:18).

9. They had become servants of righteousness (see Romans 6:18).

Believers from Rome had been at Pentecost and likely had been baptized then (Acts 2:10). Hence, the apostle Paul said to the believers, those who had already been baptized "confess and believe" (Romans 10:9-10).

Many people have read or heard this, *"for by grace you have been saved through faith"* and concluded that grace and faith excludes baptism (Ephesians 2:8). It is true that the apostle wrote this statement about the believers of Ephesus. What can we definitely know from scripture that will shed light on the subject? Let's look further.

Had not the Ephesians, those in Ephesus, heard the message of truth (Ephesians 1:13)? Had not the Ephesians, those in Ephesus, believed the message of truth?

Had not the Ephesians, those in Ephesus, been baptized? Acts 19:1-5
Those believers to whom the apostle Paul wrote, had heard the gospel, believed the gospel, and had been baptized. The grace and faith that saved them included baptism.

BECOME SAVED – Holy Spirit-led Post Resurrection Understanding of Baptism

Most of the biblical information about baptism comes after Jesus had been resurrected from the dead. The Holy Spirit guided the apostles and prophets as they spoke and wrote about baptism. Through the Holy Spirit, God provided a more comprehensive understanding of the role and relationship of baptism.

Read: Acts 8:26-40

The eunuch did not understand what he was reading from Isaiah 53:7ff (Acts 8:30-32). Philip began at Isaiah 53:7, the place where the eunuch was reading, and preached unto him Jesus (Acts 8:35).

How could Philip preach Jesus when the name Jesus is not once stated in Isaiah 53?

How could Philip demand that the eunuch believe that Jesus Christ is the Son of God when believing that Jesus Christ is the Son of God is never stated in Isaiah 53?

How could Philip introduce the subject of baptism while preaching Jesus from Isaiah 53 when baptism is not stated in Isaiah 53?
How could Philip understand Isaiah 53 when the eunuch did not?
The answers to all four questions are the same. Philip had a Holy Spirit-led post-resurrection understanding of the Old Testament scripture (Acts 6:5) and the eunuch did not.

God had more fully revealed His will to the apostles and prophets (Ephesians 3:5). There are some things that had not been understood before, but came to be understood only after the resurrection of Jesus and the coming enlightening provided through the Holy Spirit. Because Philip had a Holy Spirit-led post-resurrection understanding of the Old Testament scripture, God enlightened him to understand things more fully than did others. God enlightened His apostles and prophets to understand the Old Testament. When we read the New Testament, we gain insight into the inspired minds of the apostles and prophets (Ephesians 3:5).

Jesus recognized that men needed a post-resurrection understanding of the Old Testament scripture. Therefore, He opened their minds to understand the scriptures (Luke 24:44-47).

God opened Lydia's mind to understand (Acts 16:14). Her understanding led to her being baptized (Acts 16:15).

Where does Old Testament teach the purpose of baptism? It does not; it just illustrates it. The lamb's blood became available for the Israelites (Exodus 12:21-28). Yet, the Israelites were not free from bondage until they passed through the sea (Exodus 14:26-29). God saved Israel on the day that they passed through the water (Exodus 14:30). The Holy Spirit's inspired commentary called that experience a baptism, *"For I do not want you to be unaware, brethren, that our fathers were all under the cloud and all passed through the sea; and all were baptized into Moses in the cloud and in the sea; and all ate the same spiritual food; and all drank the same spiritual drink, for they were drinking from a spiritual rock which followed them; and the rock was Christ"* (1 Corinthians 10:1-4).

BECOME SAVED – The Dry Side of Baptism

Read: Matthew 28:18-20
When did Jesus teach about baptism, before or after salvation?

Read: Mark 16:15-18
What did Jesus say were the prerequisites of salvation?

Read: Acts 2:38
What did the apostle Peter say was the purpose of baptism?

To His apostles, Jesus made a few final remarks after His resurrection. Baptism was one of the topics that He discussed with them (Matthew 28:18-20; Mark 16:15-18). Clearly, the baptism of new believers is of vital significance to the Lord Jesus. God-fearing believers want to know that Christ approves of their baptism. Our baptism indicates that the reality of our death with Christ is a realized fact. Our baptism indicates that the reality of our death with Christ is a ruling force. Near the beginning of his ministry, the apostle Peter preached about baptism (Acts 2:38). Near the ending of his ministry, the apostle Peter wrote about baptism.

Read: 1 Peter 3:21
What does this text say that baptism does?

Indeed, the apostle Peter reminded the believers of the importance of baptism. First, we consider the "dry" side of baptism. It is a response of the mind; for it is an internal appeal toward God. The dry side is a response of the conscience. The conscience is a product of accepted teachings (John 8:1-9; Leviticus 20:10). If you have been taught to be honest and you accept that as valid, whenever you are dishonest you violate your conscience. Your conscience then causes you to feel guilty. On the other hand, if you were taught to be honest and you consider that invalid, then you do not violate your conscience. Therefore, you feel no guilt.

The dry side is a response of a **good conscience.** Within this context, a good conscience is a heart that trusts in the resurrection of Jesus Christ (1 Peter 3: 21). The resurrection proves that Jesus is the Son of God (Romans 1:4; Acts 17:31). Only those who believe in the resurrection of Jesus have a good conscience for baptism (John 8:24; Acts 8:35-37).

If one's conscience is insufficiently taught, then it will be insufficiently developed. And if one's conscience is incorrectly taught, then it will be incorrectly developed. A good conscience results from having accepted wholesome teachings. When taught insufficiently, conscience insufficiently develops (Acts 19:1-5). When taught erroneously, then conscience erroneously develops.
The Israelites, after seeing the power of God displayed through him, were baptized into Moses as their deliverer (Exodus 14:31; 1 Corinthians 10:2). We, after hearing about the power of God displayed through the resurrection of Jesus, (Romans 1:1-4) are then baptized into Christ as our Savior. To identify with Jesus and rely on Him for salvation from sin, we must be baptized.
What really happens at baptism?

John the Baptist announced that he baptized in water, but that Jesus would baptize with the Holy Spirit (Matthew 3:11; Mark. 1:8; Luke. 3:16; John 1:33). He made this statement to the general population before Jesus ever began choosing His apostles. What did he mean?

By the Holy Spirit, Jesus baptizes us all into the one body of Christ (1 Corinthians 12:13). Persons whom Jesus baptizes by the Holy Spirit are all truly members of His one body, without regard to earthly distinctions (1 Corinthians 12:13; Galatians 3:2627; Ephesians 2:18). The baptism work of the Holy Spirit has to do with the body of Christ, the church. By the Spirit baptism we are immersed into the body of Christ. Here, the Spirit is the instrument, the agent who places the believer into the body of Christ. The creation of the one body is the result of the baptism work of the Holy Spirit. At the moment of salvation, the baptism work of the Holy Spirit inducts the believer as a living member into the body of Christ. They, who are baptized by the Holy Spirit, may continue to draw refreshment and spiritual nourishment from that same inexhaustible source (John 4:1314; John 7:3739). Speaking in tongues is not the indispensable sign of the baptism work of the Holy Spirit. In the first century, even as now, every Christian experienced the baptism work of the Holy Spirit. Not even then in the first century did every Christian speak in tongues (1 Corinthians 12:30).

BECOME SAVED – The Wet Side of Baptism

Secondly, we consider the "wet" side of baptism. The wet side is a response of the body; for it is an external appeal towards God. The wet side consists of a **burial in water.**

The word "covenant" is of Latin origin. It is derived from the two words "com" = together and "venire" = to come. It meant a literal coming together.

The corresponding Hebrew word for covenant meant "to cut, to eat" as in the cutting asunder of the victims which were sacrificed at the making of a covenant (Genesis 15:9-21; Jeremiah 34:18-19). To eat, probably referred to the eating of the slain victims. To eat with someone was commonly regarded as almost equivalent to making a covenant with that person (Genesis 31:43-55; Exodus 24:1-2, 9-11).

Offering sacrifices also ratified covenants (Genesis 15:7-21; Exodus 24:3-8; Jeremiah 34:17-22). It was accepted that the sacrificial blood has the sacramental power to bind together two parties in a covenant (1 Corinthians 11:25). The Greeks had two words that conveyed the concept of covenant:
(1) *suntheke* - devoted solemn agreement made between equals
(2) *diatheke* - agreement made by superior for the acceptance and observing of an inferior

All of God's covenants are *diatheke*. A covenant must include three items: (1) covenantor, (2) covenantee, and (3) various stipulations of the contract. A covenant was a firm confirmed commitment (Hebrews 6:13-17).

Through Abram, God teaches us that commitment comes by covenant. Within each covenant there exists the core essence of the covenant and a ceremonial expression of the covenant.

God promised Abram that He would bless all the earth through him and his descendants (Genesis 12:3-5). God revealed the core essence of His covenant with Abram (Genesis 17:16; 19). He then required Abram to participate in the ceremonial expression of His covenant. Participation in the ceremonial expression of the covenant is essential to the strengthening of faith in the core essence of the covenant.

How would God have responded to Abraham if he neglected to participate in the ceremony of the covenant?

There is the ceremonial expression (ceremony) of the name change (Genesis 17:3-8; 15). God required Abram to change his and Sarai's name. There is the ceremonial expression of circumcision (Genesis 17:10-14; 23-27). God required Abraham to circumcise himself, his son and his male servants. Participation in the ceremonial expression of the covenant is essential to strengthening faith in the core essence of the covenant. Therefore, the core of the covenant is inherently attached to the ceremonial expression of the covenant. Abraham had to participate in ceremonial expression of the covenant in order to enjoy the core essence of the covenant. He could not bypass the name change and the circumcision and expect to enjoy the blessing of the covenant.

We cannot separate the two. We should not seek to separate thinking about the Lord's Supper from eating the elements (1 Corinthians 11:23-28). We cannot separate immersion from baptism (1 Peter 3:21). We cannot think the Lord's Supper into existence. We must participate in it. We cannot think baptism into existence. We must participate in it. A failure to participate in the ceremonial expression indicates ignorance or absence of integrity. The ceremonial expression of the covenant is inherently attached to the core essence of the covenant.

The term "baptism" never means sprinkle or pour, but to immerse (Acts 8:38-39; John 3:23; Matthew 27:57-60). It is not only important that baptism is practiced, but how it is practiced. It is a picture of our death, burial, and resurrection with Jesus (Romans 6:1-4). Baptism is an immersion. The fact of the definition and the fact of the illustration assure that (Acts 8:38-39). The wet side consists of a burial in water in order **to receive the benefits of the resurrection of Jesus** (1 Peter 3:21). Only when an immersion takes place for this purpose, is it valid (Acts 19:3-5).

God used the waters of the flood to save eight people during the days of Noah (1 Peter 3:20). What happens now? God uses the waters of baptism to save all who trust in the resurrection of Jesus Christ (1 Peter 3:21). The symbol preceded the real essence (Romans 5:14; Hebrews

9:24). The waters of the flood were a figure or type of baptism. Obviously, baptism consisted of that which one might think to be an external cleansing. Only if water was used, one might mistake baptism to be an external cleansing.

If you have experienced only the dry side, then you have only experienced half of a baptism. Half of a baptism is no baptism at all. You need to be immersed today. If you experienced only the wet side then there is no baptism at all. You need to be immersed today. The dry side must precede the wet side, and the wet side must follow the dry side for it to be a valid baptism. Baptism stands between you and salvation. God calls you to be baptized today.

BECOME DEVOTED – In order for a person to maximize the experience of salvation, he/she must become devoted to the instructions of the apostles. Now that you have been baptized into the body of Christ, you must learn to participate in kingdom practices so as to enjoy kingdom privileges. Always honor your kingdom citizenship.

Acts 2:41-42: On the day of Pentecost about 3,000 listeners received the word. To receive the word is to welcome the word (Luke 8:40). Those disciples who received and welcomed the word continually devoted themselves (remained faithfully in place, Acts 1:14, 2:46, 6:4, 8:13, 10:7).

They continually devoted themselves to the apostles' teachings [(doctrine, tutoring) Acts 2:42; Titus 1:9]. Teachings from the apostles originated with God (Acts 2:4; John 14:26, 7:16). Apostolic teachings were not stagnant, but were living principles that changed behavior and revolutionized the world.

They continually devoted themselves to fellowship (Acts 2:42). Through fellowship, they pledged their allegiance to each other. They expressed allegiance by participating in compatible activity because of their compatible interest (1 John 1:3, 6-7; 2 Corinthians 13:14; Philippians 2:1).

They continually devoted themselves to worship (Acts 2:42-43, 46a, 47). God wants our worship to become a matter of spiritual conviction. For us, worship should become more than just a matter of selfish convenience.

WIFE BE SUBJECT TO YOUR HUSBAND - EVEN THOUGH HE DOES NOT WANT YOU TO

Expand Your Knowledge with These Essential Reads by John Davis Marshall

"Good and Angry" - A Personal Guide to Anger Management

"The Power of the Tongue" – What You Say is What You Get

"God, Listen" – Prayers That God Always Answers [includes a 50-day addiction recovery guide]

"Final Answer"

"Success is a God Idea"

"Show Me the Money" – 7 Exercises That Build Economic Strength.

"God Knows" – There is no Need to Worry.

"My God" – Who He is Will Change Your Life.

"Faith, Family, & Finances" Vol. One –. Essential Truths That Lead to Passionate Happiness.

"Faith, Family, & Finances" Vol. Two - The Mess We are in and How to Get Out of It!

"A Queen In Search of A King" – Go Ahead and Ask Him for a Date!

"Church Matters" – Passionate Pleadings That Prepare Us For The Future

"Hallelujah" – Worship Him According to His Preference

"Called to be a Champion" – Coaching Yourself Into the Champion Circle

"Pre Marriage Preparations" – From Me to We

"Man HANDLE IT"

"Husband Love Your Wife" – Even Though She Does Not Want You To

"Wife be Subject to Your Husband" – Even Though He Does Not Want You To

"Reparations" – Break the Poverty Cycle

"Wisdom" – Things I Should Have Learned When I Was A Teenager But Didn't

www.JohnDavisMarshall.com

www.ingramcontent.com/pod-product-compliance
Lightning Source LLC
LaVergne TN
LVHW020451070526
838199LV00063B/4915